Team Spirit

THE SAN FRANCISCO GIANTS

BY

MARK STEWART

Content Consultant
James L. Gates, Jr.
Library Director
National Baseball Hall of Fame and Museum

NORWOOD HOUSE PRESS
CHICAGO, ILLINOIS

Meet the Giants

The San Francisco Giants are a hard team to ignore. Win or lose, they do things in a big way. Some of baseball's greatest hitters, pitchers, and managers have led the team. That happens when you have been putting teams on the field since the 1880s!

The players who wear the black and orange of the Giants carry a lot of *tradition* onto the field. Every day, a new page is written in one of baseball's most *remarkable* tales. Sometimes, the hero is a **slugger**, while others times fans celebrate an incredible pitching performance or a *stunning* defensive play.

This book tells the story of the Giants. It began on the East Coast in the 19th *century* and continues on the West Coast in the 21st century. One thing, however, has never changed. Wherever they play, the Giants have an amazing way of making baseball history.

Tim Lincecum enjoys a laugh in the dugout with his teammates. The Giants rely on a combination of young and old stars to build a winner.

Way Back When

In the early 1880s, a young millionaire named John B. Day wanted to be a baseball player. When he realized he would never be good enough, he did the next best thing—he bought two teams! One of those teams was the New York Gothams. They played their

TIMOTHY J. KEEFE, PITCHER.

first season in the **National League (NL)** in 1883. Jim Mutrie, Day's manager, started calling his players "giants." Soon that became the name of the team.

The Giants were the best team in baseball during the late 1880s. They were led by pitchers Tim Keefe and Mickey Welch, and hitters Buck Ewing, John Ward, and Roger Connor. The team won two **pennants** and helped baseball become the country's most popular sport.

The Giants rose to the top of the NL again in the early part of the 20th century. From 1904 to 1924, they finished first or second 16 times. Their manager during those glory years was John McGraw, who was known as the smartest man in baseball when he played. As a manager, McGraw was even smarter.

It helped to have great players, of course. And the Giants had many. Christy Mathewson, Joe McGinnity, George Wiltse, Red Ames, Rube Marquard, and Jesse Barnes were among the finest pitchers in the league. The Giants' best hitters included Roger Bresnahan, Larry Doyle, Ross

Youngs, George Kelly, Dave Bancroft, and Frankie Frisch. McGraw's teams won 10 pennants and three **World Series**.

During the 1930s, the Giants won three more pennants. They were led by hitting stars Mel Ott, Bill Terry, and Travis Jackson. Pitchers Carl Hubbell and Hal Schumacher were the top arms on the mound. After some losing seasons in the 1940s, the Giants rebuilt their club in the 1950s. They signed several stars from the **Negro Leagues**, including Monte Irvin, Hank Thompson, and Willie Mays. Many experts consider Mays to be the greatest **all-around** player of his time.

In 1958, the Giants and Brooklyn Dodgers moved to California. The Giants played in San Francisco and the Dodgers in Los

LEFT: Tim Keefe, the team's first great pitcher.   **ABOVE**: Catcher John "Chief" Meyers watches as John McGraw hits a grounder during fielding practice.

Angeles. The fierce *rivalry* they started in New York continued on the West Coast (and does to this day). With young power hitters such as Orlando Cepeda, Willie McCovey, and Felipe Alou supporting Mays—and

great pitching from Juan Marichal and Gaylord Perry—the Giants continued their winning ways in the 1960s.

The team had its ups and down for nearly two *decades*, but by the end of the 1980s, the Giants were pennant *contenders* almost every season. Their heavy hitters included Will Clark, Robby Thompson, Matt Williams, Kevin Mitchell—and later Barry Bonds and Jeff Kent. Mitchell, Bonds, and Kent each won **Most Valuable Player (MVP)** awards during this period.

San Francisco's **bullpen** starred Rod Beck and Robb Nen during the 1980s and 1990s. The only thing that kept the Giants from winning another World Series was their lack of an ace **starting pitcher**—they could not find one who could clamp down on opposing hitters. In 2002, the team won its 20th pennant but could not overcome the hot-hitting Anaheim Angels in the World Series.

LEFT: Willie Mays, who hit more than 600 home runs for the Giants in New York and San Francisco.　　**ABOVE**: Barry Bonds signs autographs for fans.

The Team Today

After reaching the World Series in 2002, the Giants started planning their return to the top of the National League. Their new manager, Felipe Alou, tried to lead a team of **veteran** players back to the pennant. Age and injuries prevented them from reaching that goal.

Barry Bonds was their greatest star, but injuries often forced him out of the **lineup**. In 2007, Bonds set the all-time record for home runs. He hit his 756th on August 7th to pass Henry Aaron. However, his time as an everyday player for the Giants was coming to an end.

History has shown that San Francisco does not waste any time trying to build a championship team. In 2007, the Giants added pitcher Barry Zito and catcher Bengie Molina. They passed along valuable advice to a lineup of young stars, including Matt Cain, Tim Lincecum, and Brian Hennessey. The Giants are **determined** to return to the top of baseball. As all of San Francisco's players know, they have more than a century of history and tradition behind them.

Catcher Bengie Molina congratulates young Brad Hennessey after a San Francisco victory. The team is at its best when it mixes youth with experience.

Home Turf

The Giants have played in three of baseball's most famous stadiums. In New York, their home was the oddly shaped Polo Grounds. A ball hit down the foul lines could travel less than 300 feet and still be a home run. A ball hit 400 feet to center field was an easy out.

After moving to San Francisco, the Giants played for 40 years in Candlestick Park. It was built right near the water and was famous for its wind and fog, especially at night.

The Giants built a new stadium in 2000. It has gone by several names, including AT&T Park. Inside and outside, the stadium reminds fans of baseball's best old-time ballparks. Their favorite feature is McCovey Cove, an area in San Francisco Bay just beyond the right field wall. Home runs hit into the water are known as "Splashdowns."

BY THE NUMBERS

- *The Giants' stadium has 41,503 seats.*
- *The distance from home plate to the left field foul pole is 339 feet.*
- *The distance from home plate to the center field fence is 399 feet.*
- *The distance from home plate to the right field foul pole is 309 feet.*

Paddlers wait for home run balls behind the stadium's right field wall.

Dressed for Success

For most of their early history, the Giants' team colors were red, white, and blue. In some years, the players wore dark blue road uniforms. In 1906, they changed to a jersey with "World's Champions" written across the front to celebrate the team's World Series victory. In 1916, the Giants wore a plaid uniform with violet stripes.

Today, the club features orange and black as its colors. They were first used in 1949, when the Giants still played in New York. Back then, the Giants often had a script *NY* on their caps and shirt sleeves. Years later, when the New York Mets came into the league, they used the same design. For the Giants, the *NY* switched to *SF*

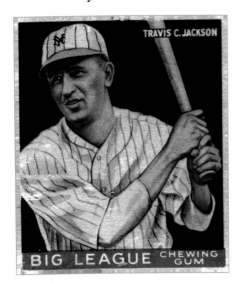

when the team moved to San Francisco in 1958. During the 1970s and 1980s, the Giants tried uniform tops that were all black or all orange. In recent years, the players have worn uniforms that look very much like the ones from the 1950s and 1960s.

Travis Jackson wears the team's blue and white uniform of the 1930s.

UNIFORM BASICS

The baseball uniform has not changed much since the Giants began playing. It has four main parts:

- a cap or batting helmet with a sun visor
- a top with a player's number on the back
- pants that reach down between the ankle and the knee
- stirrup-style socks

The uniform top sometimes has a player's name on the back. The team's name, city, or *logo* is usually on the front. Baseball teams wear light-colored uniforms when they play at home and darker styles when they play on the road.

For more than 100 years, baseball uniforms were made of wool *flannel* and were very baggy. This helped the sweat *evaporate* and gave players the freedom to move around. Today's uniforms are made of *synthetic* fabrics that stretch with players and keep them dry and cool.

Matt Cain throws a pitch during the 2007 season. The Giants have worn black and orange since the 1940s.

We Won!

The Giants were champions of baseball in 1888 and 1889. Back then, the World Series was not official, as it is today. Still, baseball's two top clubs faced off for the championship. New York won the title twice.

Pitchers Tim Keefe and Mickey Welch led those great teams. The hitting stars included Buck Ewing, Roger Connor, John Ward,

George Gore, and Mike Tiernan. In 1888 against the St. Louis Browns, Keefe pitched four complete games and allowed just two earned runs. In 1889, the Giants beat the Brooklyn Bridegrooms for the championship.

The Giants won their first modern World Series in 1905. They had baseball's most famous manager in John McGraw. He watched from the dugout as New York beat the Philadelphia Athletics four games to one. The pitching was fantastic—each game was a **shutout**! Christy Mathewson recorded three victories for the Giants.

The Giants were champions again in 1921 and 1922. Both years they met the New York Yankees in the World Series. At that time, both teams played in the Polo Grounds, so there was not much traveling to do. The Giants were led by pitchers Art Nehf and Jesse Barnes, and hitters Frankie Frisch, Ross Youngs, George Kelly, and Heinie Groh. The final game in 1921 ended on an amazing double play by the Giants' infielders.

LEFT: Christy Mathewson warms up before a game. **ABOVE**: Heinie Groh, Travis Jackson, Frankie Frisch, and George Kelly—the Giants' infield of the 1920s.

McGraw retired in 1932 and was replaced by Bill Terry, his star first baseman. The very next year, Terry guided the Giants to another championship. He and Mel Ott were the team's best hitters. Carl Hubbell and Hal Schumacher were the top pitchers. New York beat the Washington Senators four games to one.

ABOVE: Mel Ott, the team's top power hitter in the 1930s.
RIGHT: A souvenir from the 1954 World Series.

In 1954, the Giants won their fifth World Series in 50 years. Willie Mays was the star of the team. He was the most exciting all-around player in baseball—and the NL MVP that season. The Giants faced the Cleveland Indians in the World Series. Mays saved the first game with a breathtaking catch, and a **pinch-hitter** named Dusty Rhodes became a hero with three game-winning hits. The Giants swept the Indians in four games.

The Giants nearly won two more championships after moving to San Francisco in 1958. The 1962 World Series—against the Yankees—ended when the Giants left the bases loaded in the ninth inning of a 1–0 game. In the 2002 World Series—against the Angels—the Giants were ahead 5–0 late in Game Six. Anaheim scored six runs to win and force a seventh game. The next night, San Francisco led 1–0, but the Angels came back again and won 4–1.

Go-To Guys

To be a true star in baseball, you need more than a quick bat and a strong arm. You have to be a "go-to guy"—someone the manager wants on the pitcher's mound or in the batter's box when it matters most. Fans of the Giants have had a lot to cheer about over the years, including these great stars …

THE PIONEERS

WILLIAM EWING, CATCHER.

BUCK EWING   Catcher

• BORN: 10/17/1859 • DIED: 10/20/1906
• PLAYED FOR TEAM: 1883 TO 1889 & 1891 TO 1892
Buck Ewing was the best all-around player in baseball during the 1880s. He was a .300 hitter with speed and power. Just as impressive, Ewing played the *demanding* position of catcher and was one of the game's smartest men.

CHRISTY MATHEWSON   Pitcher

• BORN: 8/12/1880   • DIED: 10/7/1925   • PLAYED FOR TEAM: 1900 TO 1916
Christy Mathewson was the first true baseball "idol." He was a college-educated gentleman who won 372 games for the Giants during 17 remarkable seasons. Mathewson's best pitch was a tailing fastball that he called the "fade-away."

20   **ABOVE**: Buck Ewing   **RIGHT**: Bill Terry

BILL TERRY   First Baseman

- BORN: 10/30/1898 • DIED: 1/9/1989
- PLAYED FOR TEAM: 1923 TO 1936

Bill Terry was all business on and off the field. To him, baseball was a job— and he was very good at it. In 1930, Terry hit .401. In 1932, he became the Giants' **player-manager** and led the team to the pennant.

MEL OTT   Outfielder

- BORN: 3/2/1909 • DIED: 11/21/1958
- PLAYED FOR TEAM: 1926 TO 1947

Mel Ott went right from high school to the Giants and became the team's most beloved star for two decades. At the age of 20, he hit 42 home runs and knocked in 151 runs. Ott finished his career with 511 home runs.

CARL HUBBELL   Pitcher

- BORN: 6/22/1903 • DIED: 11/21/1988
- PLAYED FOR TEAM: 1928 TO 1943

Carl Hubbell threw baseball's best screwball—a pitch that fooled batters by moving in the opposite direction of a curveball. He won more than 20 games each year from 1933 to 1937 and was named NL MVP twice.

WILLIE MAYS   Outfielder

• BORN: 5/6/1931   • PLAYED FOR TEAM: 1951 TO 1972

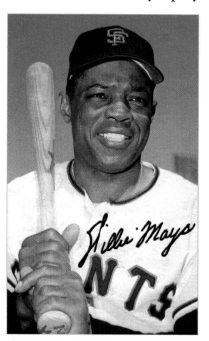

Willie Mays played baseball in a faster gear than everyone else, yet he almost never made a mistake. He was the NL's strongest hitter, best baserunner, and its most spectacular outfielder from the early 1950s to the mid-1960s. Mays retired with 660 home runs.

WILLIE McCOVEY   First Baseman/ Outfielder

• BORN: 1/10/1938

• PLAYED FOR TEAM: 1959 TO 1973 & 1977 TO 1980

No one in baseball hit the ball harder than Willie McCovey. When he swung and made contact, it sounded like a gunshot. McCovey was beloved by Giants fans. He played for the team in four decades—starting in 1959 and retiring in 1980.

JUAN MARICHAL   Pitcher

• BORN: 10/20/1937   • PLAYED FOR TEAM: 1960 TO 1973

Every pitch Juan Marichal threw was a work of art. He kicked his leg high in the air and then released the ball from any one of a dozen places. Marichal won more games in the 1960s than anyone else. Three times he posted at least 25 victories in a season.

WILL CLARK — First Baseman

- BORN: 3/13/1964 • PLAYED FOR TEAM: 1986 TO 1993

Will Clark was the heart and soul of the Giants for eight seasons in the 1980s and 1990s. His love of baseball *inspired* his teammates, and his lively bat won countless games for the team.

MATT WILLIAMS — Third Baseman

- BORN: 11/28/1965 • PLAYED FOR TEAM: 1987 TO 1996

Matt Williams was a hard-hitting, slick-fielding third baseman who powered the Giants in the 1990s. In 1994, he had a chance to break the single-season home run record before a labor dispute ended the year in August.

BARRY BONDS — Outfielder

- BORN: 7/24/1964 • PLAYED FOR TEAM: 1993 TO 2007

In 1992, Barry Bonds came "home" to the Giants. His father, Bobby, and godfather, Willie Mays, had starred for the team more than 20 years earlier. Bonds broke the single-season and career records for home runs and walks while playing for the Giants. He was also voted NL MVP each year from 2001 to 2004.

LEFT: Willie Mays
TOP RIGHT: Matt Williams
BOTTOM RIGHT: Barry Bonds

On the Sidelines

During the 1800s, the rules and *strategies* of baseball were changing all the time. A player who saw opportunities and grabbed them could become a star. John McGraw was one of the sport's smallest players, but he was also one of the smartest. After a great playing career, McGraw became the Giants' manager in 1902. He led the team for three decades. His teams finished first or second 21 times, and they won three World Series.

The Giants learned the secrets of baseball from McGraw. They were always considered one of the smartest teams in the league. Another manager who gave the Giants an edge was Leo Durocher. He reminded many fans of McGraw. Durocher led the club to pennants in 1951 and 1954.

After the Giants moved to San Francisco, several more talented managers guided the team. Alvin Dark, Charlie Fox, Roger Craig, Dusty Baker, and Felipe Alou all led the team to first-place finishes. Baker won 103 games in his first year—the most ever by a **rookie** manager.

Dusty Baker sits in the dugout with his son, Darren, who sometimes worked as the team's batboy. Baker led the Giants to the World Series in 2002.

One Great Day

There is no clock ticking during a baseball game. A team cannot win or lose until the final inning is played—and the final out is made. In 1951, the Giants and Brooklyn Dodgers battled all summer for the pennant. After 154 games, the two teams were tied with 96 wins each. The rules at the time said that the teams had to have a **playoff**—the first to win two games would be the NL champion.

The Giants won the first game 3–1 in Brooklyn's ballpark. The Dodgers won the next game 10–0. The third and final game was played on the Giants' home field, the Polo Grounds.

The game was tied after seven innings. In the top of the eighth inning, the Dodgers scored three times.

The Dodgers held a 4–1 lead in the bottom of the ninth. Brooklyn's pitcher, Don Newcombe, was exhausted. He gave up singles to Alvin Dark and Don Mueller. Monte Irvin popped out, but Whitey Lockman drilled a double that brought Dark home. The score was now 4–2.

LEFT: A pennant from New York's magical 1951 season. RIGHT: Bobby Thomson waves to the crowd moments after his famous home run.

The Dodgers brought in Ralph Branca to face Bobby Thomson. Branca threw a fastball over the plate, and Thomson watched it go by for strike one. Branca threw his next pitch high and inside. He did not expect Thomson to swing at it—he was hoping to get him out with his next pitch, a curveball.

But Thomson did swing and hit a line drive to left field. Andy Pafko of the Dodgers waited for the ball to bounce off the wall, but instead it cleared the fence. With one swing of the bat, Thomson had given the Giants a 5–4 victory!

"The Giants win the pennant! The Giants win the pennant!" cried radio announcer Russ Hodges. Thomson circled the bases and was hugged by his teammates when he reached home plate. His "shot heard 'round the world" is still one of the most famous home runs in baseball history.

Legend Has It

Who was San Francisco's first "homegrown" hero?

LEGEND HAS IT that Willie McCovey was. McCovey was the first star to begin his career in San Francisco after the team moved from New York. He joined the Giants in 1959 and was named **Rookie of the Year**. In 1962, McCovey came within a few inches of getting the winning hit in Game Seven of the World Series. In 1969, he won the NL MVP award. McCovey was the only player to wear a Giants uniform in the 1950s, 1960s, 1970s, and 1980s.

ABOVE: Willie McCovey
RIGHT: Arlie Latham

Who was baseball's first full-time coach?

LEGEND HAS IT that Arlie Latham was. In the early days of baseball, older players often helped the manager with coaching duties. In 1907, John McGraw hired Latham to help him run the Giants. Latham had been a star in the 1890s and was known for his practical jokes. He kept the Giants "loose" under the strict McGraw.

Who was the first player to use a batting helmet?

LEGEND HAS IT that Roger Bresnahan was. Bresnahan was the Giants' catcher from 1902 to 1908. He was always inventing new things for his position. One year, he made shin guards that could be strapped on the outside of his uniform. Today, all catchers wear them. Bresnahan also added a hard lining to his cap after being hit in the head with a pitch. He wore it while he hit and also while he was catching.

It Really Happened

The 1954 World Series was supposed to be a wipeout—in favor of the Cleveland Indians. No one gave the Giants a chance. The Indians had won 111 games and lost only 43—the best record in the history of the **American League (AL)**. Cleveland had great pitching and powerful hitting, and the team's manager, Al Lopez, was one of the game's best.

MAYS' CATCH MAKES SERIES HISTORY

Luckily, the Giants had Willie Mays and Dusty Rhodes. Mays was just 23 and at the beginning of his great career. He was the NL batting champ in 1954. Rhodes was mostly used as a pinch-hitter by the Giants. No one expected him to make a difference against the Indians.

The first game was tied 2–2 in the eighth inning. The Indians had two runners on base when Vic Wertz hit a long fly ball to center field. Mays turned and ran to the deepest part of the horseshoe-shaped Polo Grounds and caught the ball over his shoulder. It was the greatest catch most people had ever seen—some say the best catch ever. Mays was almost 500 feet from home plate. The Giants got two more outs to keep the game tied. Two innings later, Rhodes hit a home run to win the game.

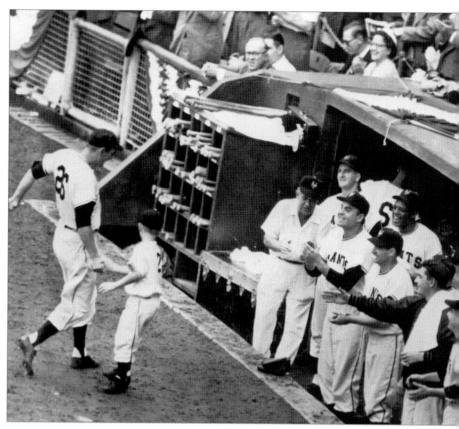

In Game Two, Rhodes pinch-hit again. He drilled a single that sent Mays home. Rhodes stayed in the game and later hit a home run. The Giants won 3–1. In Game Three, Rhodes did it again. This time his pinch-hit brought home Mays and another teammate. These were the winning runs in a 6–2 victory.

Rhodes stayed on the bench for Game Four. He watched as the Giants built a 7–0 lead and won 7–4. The 1954 World Series was a wipeout after all—but it was the Indians who took the fall.

LEFT: Willie Mays's great catch is shown on this old trading card.
ABOVE: Dusty Rhodes returns to the dugout after a pinch-hit home run.

Team Spirit

The Giants have always tried to connect with their fans. In the 1880s, their manager often roamed through the stands during games to get the crowd excited. In the 1950s, Willie Mays would often leave the ballpark after the game and play stickball with the neighborhood kids.

After moving to San Francisco in 1958, the Giants quickly connected with their new California fans. More than a million came to see them play that year—almost twice as many as they had in New York. Over the years, through many ups and downs, San Francisco fans have always cheered for their Giants.

When the Giants played in Candlestick Park, their fans were famous for their tailgating parties. Since the Giants opened their new ballpark, fans have become famous for their paddling skills. Beyond the right field wall, in McCovey Cove, a group of kayakers waits patiently to scoop up home run balls during batting practice and games.

The fans say farewell to Barry Bonds at the end of the 2007 season. They cheered him throughout a career that was filled with ups and downs.

Timeline

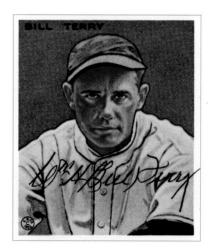

John
McGraw

MCGRAW, NEW YORK - NATIONALS

1883
The Giants join the
National League.

1903
John McGraw is hired
to manage the team.

1888
Tim Keefe wins 19 games
in a row and leads the
Giants to the pennant.

1924
The Giants become the
first NL team to win
four pennants in a row.

1930
Bill Terry is the last
National Leaguer to
bat .400 in a season.

A pennant from the early
years of the team.

GIANTS

Bill
Terry

BILL TERRY

Bobby
Bonds

1963
The Alou
brothers—Felipe,
Matty, and Jesus—
play together in the
Giants' outfield.

1974
Bobby Bonds wins
his third Gold Glove
in four seasons.

1998
Barry Bonds becomes the
first player to hit 400
homers and steal 400 bases.

1961
Willie Mays hits four
home runs in a game.

1989
The Giants reach
the World Series.

2007
Barry Bonds sets the all-
time home run record.

Will Clark pulls his son
from the stands after an
earthquake during the
1989 World Series.

Barry Bonds watches
his 756th home run
leave the ballpark.

Fun Facts

SWEET MUSIC

Songwriter Jack Norworth got the idea for "Take Me Out to the Ballgame" while riding past the Giants' stadium on a subway. He did

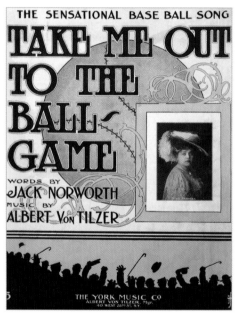

not actually go to his first baseball game until many years later.

ONE SMALL STEP FOR GAYLORD

Gaylord Perry was a good pitcher for the Giants, but a poor hitter. His manager predicted that a man would land on the moon before Perry hit a home run. In 1969, Perry hit his first homer—a few hours after Neil Armstrong stepped on the moon.

RISING SUN

In 1964 and 1965, Masanori Murakami was a member of the Giants' **pitching staff**. He was the first Japanese player in the **major leagues**.

ABOVE: "Take Me Out to the Ballgame" is sung by fans in almost every baseball stadium.　　**RIGHT**: Carl Hubbell

KING CARL

In the 1934 **All-Star Game**, Carl Hubbell struck out five batters in a row—Babe Ruth, Lou Gehrig, Jimmie Foxx, Al Simmons, and Joe Cronin. All five later joined Hubbell in the **Hall of Fame**.

TIME ON HIS SIDE

In 2004, 40-year-old Barry Bonds became the oldest player in any North American sports league to be named Most Valuable Player.

HONOR ROLL

More than 50 Hall of Famers have worn the Giants' uniform over the years. Willie Mays (2,857) and Mel Ott (2,730) played the most games. Dan Brouthers (2) and Steve Carlton (6) played the fewest.

BAT MAN

For a few days in October 1987, San Francisco's Jeffrey Leonard was the best player on earth. He batted .417 with four home runs against the St. Louis Cardinals in the **National League Championship Series (NLCS)**. Even though the Giants lost, Leonard was named MVP of the series.

Talking Baseball

"I don't compare 'em … I just catch 'em."
—*Willie Mays, on which of his catches was the greatest*

"There's nothing tough about playing third. All a guy needs is a strong arm and a strong chest."
—*Frankie Frisch, on moving from second base to the "hot corner" for the Giants*

"There is only one game, and that game is baseball."
—*John McGraw, on which sport is the best*

"I've always played for the acceptance of my godfather and father."
—*Barry Bonds, on looking up to Willie Mays and his father, Bobby Bonds*

"There's no place I'd rather be than right here. It's a good blend of the familiar and change."
—*Barry Zito, on joining the Giants after playing many years in nearby Oakland*

"As long as I've got one chance to beat you, I'm going to take it."
—*Leo Durocher, on being a good manager*

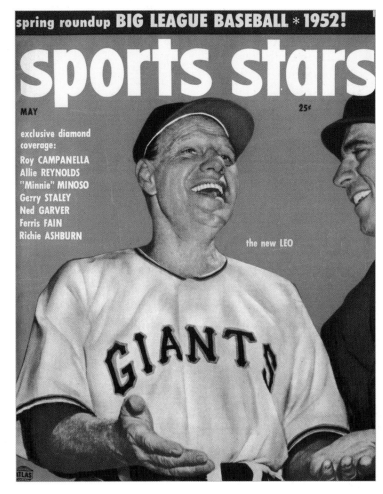

spring roundup **BIG LEAGUE BASEBALL ★ 1952!**

sports stars

MAY 25¢

exclusive diamond coverage:
Roy CAMPANELLA
Allie REYNOLDS
"Minnie" MINOSO
Gerry STALEY
Ned GARVER
Ferris FAIN
Richie ASHBURN

the new LEO

GIANTS

"Baseball has done more to move America in the right direction than all the professional patriots with all their cheap words."
—*Monte Irvin, on the role baseball has played in equality and civil rights*

LEFT: Frankie Frisch
ABOVE: Leo Durocher

For the Record

The great Giants teams and players have left their marks on the record books. These are the "best of the best" …

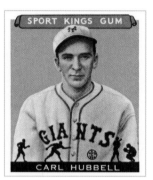

Carl Hubbell

Juan Marichal

GIANTS AWARD WINNERS

WINNER	AWARD	YEAR
Carl Hubbell	Most Valuable Player	1933
Carl Hubbell	Most Valuable Player	1936
Willie Mays	Rookie of the Year	1951
Dusty Rhodes	World Series MVP	1954
Willie Mays	Most Valuable Player	1954
Orlando Cepeda	Rookie of the Year	1958
Willie McCovey	Rookie of the Year	1959
Willie Mays	All-Star Game MVP	1963
Juan Marichal	All-Star Game MVP	1965
Willie Mays	Most Valuable Player	1965
Mike McCormick	Cy Young Award*	1967
Willie Mays	All-Star Game MVP	1968
Willie McCovey	All-Star Game MVP	1969
Willie McCovey	Most Valuable Player	1969
Bobby Bonds	All-Star Game MVP	1973
Gary Matthews	Rookie of the Year	1973
John Montefusco	Rookie of the Year	1975
Kevin Mitchell	Most Valuable Player	1989
Dusty Baker	Manager of the Year	1993
Barry Bonds	Most Valuable Player	1993
Dusty Baker	Manager of the Year	1997
Dusty Baker	Manager of the Year	2000
Jeff Kent	Most Valuable Player	2000
Barry Bonds	Most Valuable Player	2001
Barry Bonds	Most Valuable Player	2002
Barry Bonds	Most Valuable Player	2003
Barry Bonds	Most Valuable Player	2004

The annual trophy given to each league's best pitcher.

GIANTS ACHIEVEMENTS

ACHIEVEMENT	YEAR
NL Pennant Winners	1888
World Series Champions	1888
NL Pennant Winners	1889
World Series Champions	1889
NL Pennant Winners	1904
NL Pennant Winners	1905
World Series Champions	1905
NL Pennant Winners	1911
NL Pennant Winners	1912
NL Pennant Winners	1913
NL Pennant Winners	1917
NL Pennant Winners	1921
World Series Champions	1921
NL Pennant Winners	1922
World Series Champions	1922
NL Pennant Winners	1923
NL Pennant Winners	1924
NL Pennant Winners	1933
World Series Champions	1933
NL Pennant Winners	1936
NL Pennant Winners	1937
NL Pennant Winners	1951
NL Pennant Winners	1954
World Series Champions	1954
NL Pennant Winners	1962
NL West Champions	1971
NL West Champions	1987
NL West Champions	1989
NL Pennant Winners	1989
NL West Champions	1997
NL West Champions	2000
NL Wild Card	2002
NL Pennant Winners	2002
NL West Champions	2003

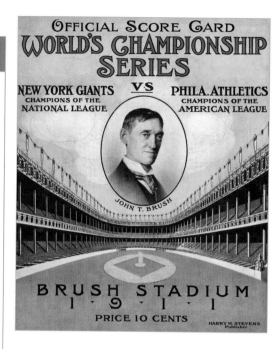

ABOVE: A program from the 1911 World Series.
BELOW: Dusty Baker, manager of the 2002 pennant winners.

Pinpoints

The history of a baseball team is made up of many smaller stories. These stories take place all over the map—not just in the city a team calls "home." Match the pushpins on these maps to the Team Facts and you will begin to see the story of the Giants unfold!

TEAM FACTS

1   San Francisco, California—*The Giants have played here since 1958.*

2   Sioux City, Iowa—*Dave Bancroft was born here.*

3   Cleveland, Ohio—*Rube Marquard was born here.*

4   Factoryville, Pennsylvania—*Christy Mathewson was born here.*

5   New York, New York—*The Giants played here from 1883 to 1957.*

6   Carthage, Missouri—*Carl Hubbell was born here.*

7   Williamston, North Carolina—*Gaylord Perry was born here.*

8   Atlanta, Georgia—*Bill Terry was born here.*

9   Westfield, Alabama—*Willie Mays was born here.*

10 West Palm Beach, Florida—*Robby Thompson was born here.*

11 Laguna Verde, Dominican Republic—*Juan Marichal was born here.*

12 Glasgow, Scotland—*Bobby Thomson was born here.*

Dave Bancroft

Play Ball

Baseball is a game played between two teams over nine innings. Teams take one turn at bat and one turn in the field during each inning. A turn at bat ends when three outs are made. The batters on the hitting team try to reach base safely. The players on the fielding team try to prevent this from happening.

In baseball, the ball is controlled by the pitcher. The pitcher must throw the ball to the batter, who decides whether or not to swing at each pitch. If a batter swings and misses, it is a strike. If the batter lets a good pitch go by, it is also a strike. If the batter swings and the ball does not stay in fair territory (between the v-shaped lines that begin at home plate) it is called "foul," and is counted as a strike. If the pitcher throws three strikes, the batter is out. If the pitcher throws four bad pitches before that, the batter is awarded first base. This is called a base-on-balls, or "walk."

When the batter swings the bat and hits the ball, everyone springs into action. If a fielder catches a batted ball before it hits the ground, the batter is out. If a fielder scoops the ball off the ground and throws it to first base before the batter arrives, the batter is out. If the batter reaches first base safely, he is credited with a hit. A one-base hit is called a single, a two-base hit is called a double, a three-base hit is called a triple, and a four-base hit is called a home run.

Runners who reach base are only safe when they are touching one of the bases. If they are caught between the bases, the fielders can tag them with the ball and record an out.

A batter who is able to circle the bases and make it back to home plate before three outs are made is credited with a run scored. The team with the most runs after nine innings is the winner.

Anyone who has played baseball (or softball) knows that it can be a complicated game. Every player on the field has a job to do. Different players have different strengths and weaknesses. The pitchers, batters, and managers make hundreds of decisions every game. The more you play and watch baseball, the more "little things" you are likely to notice. The next time you are at a game, look for these plays:

PLAY LIST

DOUBLE PLAY—A play where the fielding team is able to make two outs on one batted ball. This usually happens when a runner is on first base, and the batter hits a ground ball to one of the infielders. The base runner is forced out at second base and the ball is then thrown to first base before the batter arrives.

HIT AND RUN—A play where the runner on first base sprints to second base while the pitcher is throwing the ball to the batter. When the second baseman or shortstop moves toward the base to wait for the catcher's throw, the batter tries to hit the ball to the place that the fielder has just left. If the batter swings and misses, the fielding team can tag the runner out.

INTENTIONAL WALK—A play when the pitcher throws four bad pitches on purpose, allowing the batter to walk to first base. This happens when the pitcher would much rather face the next batter—and is willing to risk putting a runner on base.

SACRIFICE BUNT—A play where the batter makes an out on purpose so that a teammate can move to the next base. On a bunt, the batter tries to "deaden" the pitch with the bat instead of swinging at it.

SHOESTRING CATCH—A play where an outfielder catches a short hit an inch or two above the ground, near the tops of his shoes. It is not easy to run as fast as you can and lower your glove without slowing down. It can be risky, too. If a fielder misses a shoestring catch, the ball might roll all the way to the fence.

Glossary

BASEBALL WORDS TO KNOW

ALL-AROUND—Good at all parts of the game.

ALL-STAR GAME—Baseball's annual game featuring the best players from the American League and National League.

AMERICAN LEAGUE (AL)—One of baseball's two major leagues; the AL began play in 1901.

BULLPEN—The area where a team's relief pitchers warm up; this word also describes the group of relief pitchers in this area.

HALL OF FAME—The museum in Cooperstown, New York, where baseball's greatest players are honored. A player voted into the Hall of Fame is sometimes called a "Hall of Famer."

LINEUP—The list of players who are playing in a game.

MAJOR LEAGUES—The top level of professional baseball leagues. The American League and National League make up today's major leagues.

MOST VALUABLE PLAYER (MVP)—An annual award given to each league's top player; an MVP is also selected for the World Series and All-Star Game.

NATIONAL LEAGUE (NL)—The older of the two major leagues; the NL began play in 1876.

NATIONAL LEAGUE CHAMPIONSHIP SERIES (NLCS)—The competition that has decided the National League pennant since 1969.

NEGRO LEAGUES—Baseball leagues organized and run by African-Americans. Major League Baseball did not welcome black players until 1947.

PENNANTS—League championships. The term comes from the triangular flag awarded to each season's champion, beginning in the 1870s.

PINCH-HITTER—A player who is sent into the game to hit for a teammate.

PITCHING STAFF—The group of players who pitch for a team.

PLAYER-MANAGER—A player who also manages his team.

PLAYOFF—A series played after the regular season to determine which teams will have a chance to advance to the World Series.

ROOKIE—Someone in his first season.

ROOKIE OF THE YEAR—An annual award given to each league's best first-year player.

SHUTOUT—A game in which one team does not allow its opponent to score a run.

SLUGGER—A powerful hitter.

STARTING PITCHER—The pitcher who begins the game for his team.

WORLD SERIES—The world championship series played between the winners of the National League and American League.

OTHER WORDS TO KNOW

CENTURY—A period of 100 years.

CONTENDERS—People who compete for a championship.

DECADES—Periods of 10 years; also specific periods, such as the 1950s.

DEMANDING—Requiring great effort.

DETERMINED—Showing great desire.

EVAPORATE—Disappear, or turn into vapor.

FLANNEL—A soft wool or cotton material.

INSPIRED—Gave positive and confident feelings to others.

LOGO—A symbol or design that represents a company or team.

REMARKABLE—Unusual or exceptional.

RIVALRY—An extremely emotional competition.

STRATEGIES—Plans or methods for succeeding.

STUNNING—Amazing or astonishing.

SYNTHETIC—Made in a laboratory, not in nature.

TRADITION—A belief or custom that is handed down from generation to generation.

VETERAN—Having many years of experience.

Places to Go

ON THE ROAD

SAN FRANCISCO GIANTS
24 Willie Mays Plaza
San Francisco, California 94107
(408) 297-1435

NATIONAL BASEBALL HALL OF FAME AND MUSEUM
25 Main Street
Cooperstown, New York 13326
(888) 425-5633
www.baseballhalloffame.org

ON THE WEB

THE SAN FRANCISCO GIANTS www.sanfranciscogiants.com
  • *Learn more about the Giants*

MAJOR LEAGUE BASEBALL www.mlb.com
  • *Learn more about all the major league teams*

MINOR LEAGUE BASEBALL www.minorleaguebaseball.com
  • *Learn more about the minor leagues*

ON THE BOOKSHELF

To learn more about the sport of baseball, look for these books at your library or bookstore:

  • Kelly, James. *Baseball.* New York, New York: DK, 2005.

  • Jacobs, Greg. *The Everything Kids' Baseball Book.* Cincinnati, Ohio: Adams Media Corporation, 2006.

  • Stewart, Mark and Kennedy, Mike. *Long Ball: The Legend and Lore of the Home Run.* Minneapolis, Minnesota: Millbrook Press, 2006.

Index

The Team

MARK STEWART has written more than 25 books on baseball, and over 100 sports books for kids. He grew up in New York City during the 1960s rooting for the Yankees and Mets, and now takes his two daughters, Mariah and Rachel, to the same ballparks. Mark comes from a family of writers. His grandfather was Sunday Editor of the *New York Times* and his mother was Articles Editor of *Ladies' Home Journal* and *McCall's*. Mark has profiled hundreds of athletes over the last 20 years. He has also written several books about his native New York and New Jersey, his home today. Mark is a graduate of Duke University, with a degree in history. He lives with his daughters and wife, Sarah, overlooking Sandy Hook, NJ.

JAMES L. GATES, JR. has served as Library Director at the National Baseball Hall of Fame since 1995. He had previously served in academic libraries for almost fifteen years. He holds degrees from Belmont Abbey College, the University of Notre Dame, and Indiana University. During his career Jim has authored several academic articles and has served in an editorial capacity on multiple book, magazine, and museum publications, and he also serves as host for the Annual Cooperstown Symposium on Baseball and American Culture. He is an ardent Baltimore Orioles fan and enjoys watching baseball with his wife and two children.